W9-ARB-942

ARABIAN NIGHT

Roland Schimmelpfennig

ARABIAN NIGHT

Translated by David Tushingham

OBERON BOOKS
LONDON

WWW.OBERONBOOKS.COM

First published in English in 2002 by Oberon Books Ltd.
521 Caledonian Road, London N7 9RH
Tel: 020 7607 3637 / Fax: 020 7607 3629
e-mail: info@oberonbooks.com
www.oberonbooks.com

Reprinted in 2011.

A catalogue record for this book is available from the British
Library.

ISBN: 978-1-84002-298-8

Printed in Great Britain by CPI Antony Rowe, Chippenham.

Characters

HANS LOMEIER

FATIMA MANSUR

FRANZISKA DEHKE

KALIL

PETER KARPATI

Arabian Night was first performed in the United Kingdom at the The Bull, Barnet on 10 April 2002 with the following cast:

HANS LOMEIER: Sam Cox
FATIMA MANSUR: Stephanie Street
FRANZISKA DEHKE: Anna Hope
KALIL: Akbar Kurta
PETER KARPATI: Mark Benson

Creative team

Director: Gordon Anderson
Designer: Es Devlin
Assistant Designer: Lisa Lillywhite
Lighting Designer: Nigel Edwards
Sound Designer: Joff White
Production Manager: Simon Sturgess
Company Stage Manager: Lee Drinkwater
Executive Producer: Emma Dunton
Administrator: Judith Kilvington
Associate Director: Rebecca Manson Jones

LOMEIER: I can hear water. There isn't any but I can
hear it. In the middle of June. It's hot. I get phone
calls from the eighth, ninth and tenth floors: what's
happened to the water. I don't know. I've been down to
the cellar. The pressure's fine. But from the eighth floor
up all the taps are dry. On the eighth, ninth and tenth
floors there's no water at all. Like the water's got lost
on the seventh floor somewhere. There could be a leak.
But it's hard to imagine. A leak that size, a broken pipe,
would be pretty hard to miss. There'd be water running
down the walls, on all the floors, in the corridors.
But I can hear water. I can hear it through the walls.
Climbing. It sounds like singing. There's a faint singing
in the corridors. Singing on the stairs. A trail leading to
the seventh floor. I get in the lift. I'm going up to the
seventh floor to have a look. I keep on hearing water.
The lift sounds like it's going to break down again.
Seventh floor. On my right fifteen flats and the lift;
on my left, sixteen flats. All three rooms plus kitchen
and bathroom. At the end of the corridor to the right,
outside 7–32, is Franziska Dehke's Arab lodger, Fatima
Mansur. 7–32 means the kitchen window and balcony
are south-east facing, and the bathroom faces west. The
girl's trying to get the door open carrying three bags of
shopping, but why's she making such a meal of it? Why
doesn't she just put the stuff down?

FATIMA: The lift sounded like it's going to break down
again. Getting the door open carrying three bags of
shopping's not easy. Can't do it.

LOMEIER: She drops the key – better than dropping the
bags.

FATIMA: The key falls down but I can reach the bell with
my elbow. I hope Franziska's in. 'Course she's in. I hope

she hears the bell. Lomeier, the caretaker, comes down the corridor with that grey overall of his on. It's hot.

LOMEIER: She rings the bell again. She does this by resting her elbow on it then leaning in with her weight and the weight of the shopping. Can I help?

FATIMA: It's alright thanks. Hot or what?

LOMEIER: Hottest day of the year so far, it said on the seven o'clock news.

FATIMA: Still working then, Mr Lomeier?

LOMEIER: I don't know – there's something wrong with the water pressure on the eighth, ninth and tenth floors.

FATIMA: Good job there's only ten floors, eh. He doesn't laugh.

LOMEIER: Yeah.

FATIMA: He looks distant. Preoccupied.

LOMEIER: Is your water alright?

FATIMA: Well, I don't know – I only just got here. If there is anything, I'll let you know.

LOMEIER: Yeah, please, do. We might have a leak somewhere. She rings the bell again, but no-one answers. Excuse me.

FATIMA: He bends down and picks up my key. He's going to give it to me but then he realises I've still got both hands full so he just stands there not knowing what to do.

LOMEIER: She's got so many keys here.

FATIMA: I smile. What else can I do – he's looking at my keys.

LOMEIER: So many…

FATIMA: Would you mind – ? I make room for him – It's the one with the camel on.

LOMEIER: The camel is a battered, not especially attractive plastic key fob.

FATIMA: He puts the key in the lock –

LOMEIER: Would you mind me checking your water? Just to make sure it's okay.

FATIMA: No, no, not at all –

LOMEIER: Just as I'm about to turn the key in the lock, someone opens the door from inside. Standing before us, covered in sweat and with very little on, is Franziska Dehke, tenant of 7–32. Oh –

FRANZISKA: Ah – I thought I could hear something. Hello.

LOMEIER: Good afternoon.

FRANZISKA: Afternoon.

LOMEIER: Perhaps I'd better come back later –

FATIMA: If you want. Didn't you hear me? That's three times I've rung –

LOMEIER: She rests against the door with her shopping.

FRANZISKA: I don't know – I was on the sofa, having a lie down.

LOMEIER: Her key's still in the door. I take it out of the lock and give it to her.

FATIMA: He gives me the key, I wedge it against one of the shopping bags with a finger. Thanks again and do pop back later about the missing water.

LOMEIER: Yeah, I might do that. Well have a nice evening –

FATIMA: In the hall now with the shopping – Thanks! Shut the door. Can't keep hold of the keys any longer and they fall on the floor.

LOMEIER: Shuts the door. Sounds like she's just dropped the keys again.

FATIMA: I put the bags down in the kitchen.

LOMEIER: By the bell it says Franziska Dehke. The plastic's all yellow. Just handwriting. Never been cared for. She's lived there for years.

FATIMA: Why didn't you open the door?

FRANZISKA: I did –

FATIMA: Yeah but when? Franziska goes back into the living room.

FRANZISKA: Must have fallen asleep, I suppose. On the sofa. It's so hot.

FATIMA: Draw the curtains then –

FRANZISKA: 'S no point. I'm going to have a shower.

FATIMA: You better – upstairs they haven't got any water.

FRANZISKA: Uh?

FATIMA: 'T's why Lomeier was here.

LOMEIER: Or should I've just gone straight in there? No. She hardly had any clothes on.

FATIMA: She always does this.

LOMEIER: Her face was all red. And her short, blonde hair covered in sweat. Can't go barging in like that.

FATIMA: She comes home from work at the lab, takes her clothes off and lies down on the sofa. She feels tired. And then she goes and has a shower.

FRANZISKA: I can't believe I'm this tired. Shall I have a shower or not?

FATIMA: Go on.

FRANZISKA: Yeah, I suppose. But what have I been doing all day?

FATIMA: She stands there in the hall unable to make up her mind, she's wondering.

LOMEIER: Everyone's coming home from work wanting to cook supper. Or have a shower. How are they going to do that without any water?

FRANZISKA: I can't decide. Do you want a drink?

FATIMA: No thanks, I'll get these bags emptied first.

FRANZISKA: I'll pour you one anyway.

FATIMA: Go and have your shower – She walks back to the sofa.

FRANZISKA: Dunno.

FATIMA: Go on –

FRANZISKA: Okay, alright –

KALIL: Almost eight-thirty. The phone should ring any moment now.

LOMEIER: Almost eight-thirty. I'm standing by the lift wondering whether I should knock at 7–32 again.

FATIMA: The brandy bottle's on the little table by the sofa.

FRANZISKA: There's not much left in here.

FATIMA: Got a new one. She pours herself one.

LOMEIER: No. I can't go back now.

KALIL: She'll phone soon. I sit beside it waiting. I know she's going to phone. She phones every night. I love her.

FATIMA: She stands in the doorway with her glass of brandy and doesn't know where she's going.

LOMEIER: It's better if I phone them a bit later then come back up and have a look.

FRANZISKA: I think I will have a shower.

KALIL: She phones every night. Always before sunset.

FATIMA: You sure?

FRANZISKA: Yeah, I think I will.

KALIL: I look out of the window and wait for her to phone.

LOMEIER: The lift's coming. It's too slow. My eyes wander back down the corridor, up and down the walls. I can hear water. It's everywhere.

FATIMA: She turns away.

KALIL: Why hasn't she phoned?

FATIMA: And then turns back to face me again.

FRANZISKA: Weird.

FATIMA: What is it?

FRANZISKA: What have I been doing all day?

FATIMA: Working?

FRANZISKA: Probably.

FATIMA: Look – go and get in the shower –

FRANZISKA: Just I can't remember anything –

FATIMA: Oh, come on –

FRANZISKA: Well –

LOMEIER: The lift door opens.

FRANZISKA: I'm going.

FATIMA: You do that.

KALIL: The sun is low down in the West. The telephone doesn't ring.

FATIMA: Time to phone.

LOMEIER: Should I get in?

FRANZISKA: Should I really have a shower?

KALIL: Is she still going to phone?

FATIMA: Are you going for a shower now?

FRANZISKA: Er, yes –

LOMEIER: I decide to take the stairs.

FRANZISKA: Yes –

FATIMA: She goes into the bathroom. I pick up the phone.

LOMEIER: I walk down. Singing seems to fill the whole stairwell.

FATIMA: Are you going to come?

KALIL: Yeah, course –

FATIMA: Just wait –

KALIL: I know –

FATIMA: Till it gets dark.

KALIL: I know – see you.

FATIMA: See you.

LOMEIER: Sixth floor.

KARPATI: Evening approaches. I look out of the window at Block C opposite. A beam of blinding light hits my eye. The bathroom window of one of the flats on the seventh floor has been propped wide open. The evening sun is reflecting in the door of the little cupboard over the sink as it sets low in the West. I can even make out the toothbrushes in the cup next to the tap. A woman with short, blonde hair comes into the bathroom.

FATIMA: She's in the bathroom. This happens every evening before sunset. She comes home. She takes her clothes off, gets tired. All of a sudden she can't remember a thing about the day that's just gone.

FRANZISKA: I'm standing in the bathroom. Next to the sink with the toothbrushes in a plastic cup.

KARPATI: She's only wearing underwear. She takes it off and gets in the bath. She turns the water on and starts taking a shower.

FATIMA: She's having a shower.

LOMEIER: Fifth floor. I can hear water.

KALIL: She's phoned. Soon it'll be dark and I can go to her.

FRANZISKA: Cool water runs down my back.

KARPATI: They've got water, that's funny. Here in Block B there hasn't been any for the last two hours. Perhaps the pipe that feeds off the main has broken. Unusual, specially at this time of year.

FATIMA: She has a shower every evening after she comes home. She likes long showers, really long.

KARPATI: She sits in the bath having a shower. Staring in front of her. She doesn't seem to notice that the window's wide open. She just carries on with her shower, all I can see is her head and occasionally her right arm.

LOMEIER: Fourth floor.

FRANZISKA: I sit in the bathtub staring in front of me. What did I do all day?

FATIMA: I can hear the water running in the bathroom.

KARPATI: It's not the woman washing that keeps me at the window. There's something strange. A sound.

FRANZISKA: The window's open –

FATIMA: She comes home from work, she works in a laboratory, and from the moment she steps through the door with each passing second the day that's just gone recedes further and further into the distance until by sunset she can't even remember her own name.

KARPATI: I can hear water.

KALIL: I put the keys in my pocket and pick up my helmet.

KARPATI: Is that possible? Is it coming from outside? I open the window –

LOMEIER: Third floor.

FRANZISKA: In the building opposite, on the shady side of Block B, a window opens on the seventh floor.

KARPATI: It's not coming from outside.

FRANZISKA: A man leans out of the window, he seems to be looking for something.

KARPATI: Sounds like singing.

FRANZISKA: What could that be?

KARPATI: It's not inside either – Water.

FRANZISKA: Can he see me? Don't think so.

KALIL: I start the moped.

FRANZISKA: What have I been doing all day?

FATIMA: It's been like this the whole time we've been here. We've lived here together for four years now. Every night at sunset she falls fast asleep on the sofa. Then my boyfriend comes, Kalil. She doesn't know him, she doesn't suspect a thing, because she's always asleep when he comes to see me.

LOMEIER: Second floor.

KALIL: I've known her for two years now. She's the only woman in my life. I'd never be unfaithful to her. Never.

FRANZISKA: He shuts the window again. The glass reflects the deep blue of the evening sky. I don't think he can see me.

KARPATI: She turns the water off. Stands up. Gets dried.

FATIMA: I've never told her about him.

FRANZISKA: I dry myself, wrap a towel around me and leave.

FATIMA: Why not?

KARPATI: She goes out of the bathroom.

FATIMA: No idea.

KALIL: It's always like this. I've got to wait till sunset, then I can go to her. I get on my moped and go there. To her little flat. She's by the door expecting me. Her flatmate Franziska's lying asleep on the sofa. She never wakes up. She doesn't know me, she's never seen me. She doesn't even know I exist.

LOMEIER: First floor.

FATIMA: Was it nice then?

FRANZISKA: Mmhm.

FATIMA: D'you want the sofa?

FRANZISKA: The sun's almost gone.

FATIMA: A splash more brandy?

FRANZISKA: Ah –

FATIMA: She yawns. How d'it go today?

FRANZISKA: Today?

FATIMA: Yeah –

FRANZISKA: Where?

FATIMA: At work?

KARPATI: Now the sun's gone. But I can still hear this sound – the sound of water, as if I can still hear her in the shower.

FRANZISKA: What work? What are you talking about?

FATIMA: Her eyes fall shut.

LOMEIER: Ground floor. Downstairs.

KALIL: The moped's headlight stretches out on the road ahead of me. It's warm. I can already see the flats in the distance. Soon I'll be there.

LOMEIER: Purely out of curiosity I press the button for the lift on the ground floor.

KARPATI: The singing leads me out of the flat, pulling me towards her, across to Block C, to the seventh floor.

LOMEIER: I knew it. I press the button for the lift and nothing happens. The lift's on the seventh floor not going anywhere. Knackered. Well and truly.

FATIMA: You asleep?

FRANZISKA: Mmh?

FATIMA: Are you asleep yet?

FRANZISKA: What?

FATIMA: Asked if you were asleep.

FRANZISKA: Leave me –

KARPATI: Out of the flat – I've got to go to her.

FATIMA: She won't wake again now till dawn. Then she'll be wide awake, she'll make Turkish coffee, wake me up, Good Morning Fatima, my Oriental princess, I've got to dash I'll be late for work, but listen, I must have gone to sleep on the sofa again last night, why didn't you wake me up? I wonder what would happen if one night she did wake up.

KARPATI: I go down the corridor to the lift. I've got to talk to her.

FATIMA: If someone succeeded in waking her.

KARPATI: The lift is already up here. I've got to tell her about the singing. I open the metal door with the little window, get inside the lift, press G. Its inner door rattles shut and I start going down.

FATIMA: Maybe someone'd need to come and kiss her awake.

KARPATI: Six, five. It sounds like being in a Turkish bath. Four, three.

KALIL: The flats are getting closer. More homes than you can count with lights on behind the curtains. That's where Fatima lives, up there.

KARPATI: Two, one.

LOMEIER: I walk along the corridor to my flat in the basement. At the door I hear the voice of the woman who used to be my wife.

KARPATI: Ground floor. I get out of the lift and cross the lawn between the two buildings. It's dark now. There are lights on in the windows. People have left their balcony doors open.

LOMEIER: I remember her way of talking.

KARPATI: I stand in front of the entrance to Block C and look up seven floors.

FATIMA: If someone did come and kiss her maybe that would mean the end of these nights, nights with her sleeping on the sofa while I sit beside her watching TV or I'm with Kalil.

KARPATI: The main door's been left open.

LOMEIER: How long is it since I thought about her –

KARPATI: Shall I take the lift or the stairs? Water's running in the walls, I can hear it. I follow the sound – and start climbing the stairs.

KALIL: I'm almost there.

FATIMA: I can hear Kalil's moped outside.

LOMEIER: Where did that come from all of a sudden?

KARPATI: First floor.

KALIL: I know she can already hear my moped.

FATIMA: That's him.

LOMEIER: Don't think about it.

KALIL: I rev the engine up again in neutral, before switching it off in front of the entrance. I lock my helmet onto the luggage rack like I always do.

LOMEIER: Just don't think about it.

KALIL: I stand in front of the building and look up seven floors. That's where she lives, up there.

FATIMA: Now he'll get the lift straight up.

KALIL: The main door's been left open.

KARPATI: Second floor.

KALIL: Shall I take the lift or the stairs? I stand there undecided next to the green metal door to the lift.

LOMEIER: I can see her right in front of me talking to me.

KALIL: I press the button for the lift. Nothing happens. I press it again. Now.

FATIMA: Right now.

KALIL: The lift's coming down. Sounds strange.

KARPATI: Third floor.

FATIMA: Franziska's asleep.

LOMEIER: Forget it.

KALIL: Here it comes. The inner door opens. I open the metal door with the little window and get in. Press seven. Maximum load 300 kilos or five persons. Built 1972, Lübbes and Peters.

LOMEIER: Just forget about it.

KALIL: The inner door rattles shut. The lift goes up. First floor.

FATIMA: I go to the door –

KALIL: Second floor. The motor sounds odd. Third floor.

KARPATI: Fourth floor.

KALIL: Fourth floor. I don't believe it. Just under the fifth floor the lift's stopped. It's stuck.

LOMEIER: Can't.

FATIMA: Where is he?

KALIL: The lift's not moving. I do not fucking believe it. Nothing works. Not even the alarm.

LOMEIER: Now it occurs to me: I ought to put a sign up on the lift: OUT OF ORDER. So people don't spend hours hanging around wondering why it won't come.

KALIL: I'm going to go mad. Hel-lo?

LOMEIER: Take that thing off, you're at home now, she would have said.

KARPATI: Fifth floor. I'm really excited.

KALIL: Can anybody hear me?

LOMEIER: And I better phone the engineer from Lübbes and Peters.

FATIMA: It was definitely his moped. I go out onto the balcony and look down. Yep, there it is – with his red helmet locked onto the luggage rack as usual. So where's Kalil?

KALIL: Hel-lo?

LOMEIER: But there's no need to call him today. As long as the lift's stuck on the seventh floor, no harm can be done.

FATIMA: I go out of the flat, leave the front door open and head down the corridor. Kalil? He can't have –

KARPATI: Sixth floor.

FATIMA: The lift's not moving. He must be coming up the stairs. I go down to meet him.

KALIL: Hello? Nobody can hear me.

FATIMA: I can hear footsteps – that'll be him.

KARPATI: Someone's coming down.

FATIMA: No, it isn't him, it's somebody else.

KARPATI: An Arab-looking woman eyes me nervously then dashes past down the stairs.

FATIMA: Never seen him before.

LOMEIER: You know I don't like that overall.

FATIMA: Sixth floor.

KALIL: If Fatima heard my moped, she'll wonder where I am and come looking for me. Hello?

KARPATI: Seventh floor. I've made it. The woman in the shower's flat must be at the end of the corridor. I've no idea what I'm going to say when she opens the door.

LOMEIER: She paused. I never liked it.

KALIL: Fatima?

FATIMA: Fifth floor.

LOMEIER: I'll go back up and have another look. Pop up there and ask Franziska if I can just check the pipes.

KARPATI: I run along the corridor. There's a rushing in my ears.

KALIL: What if nobody finds me?

FATIMA: Fourth floor. I'm running down the stairs. Kalil?

LOMEIER: Better to do it sooner rather than later –

KARPATI: The door's open.

LOMEIER: Maybe I should leave it a while – she had practically nothing on.

KALIL: Can anybody hear me?

FATIMA: Third floor.

KARPATI: The door to the flat is wide open –

FATIMA: Kalil? Where are you?

KARPATI: Hello?

KALIL: Hello?

FATIMA: Hello? Second floor.

LOMEIER: I'll go a bit later. That'll be better.

KARPATI: Is anyone there? I step inside the flat.

LOMEIER: Won't it?

KALIL: I press every button in the lift repeatedly. Useless.

FATIMA: First floor.

KARPATI: My heart's thumping.

FATIMA: I'm out of breath. Ground floor. I remember I've left the door to the flat open upstairs.

KARPATI: There she is. Lying on the sofa asleep. She looks gorgeous. She's in a deep sleep. I can hear water rushing in my ears, and singing in my head, getting clearer all the time.

KALIL: It's hopeless.

FATIMA: No Kalil. This isn't happening. I walk outside onto the little forecourt. That's his moped over there – there's a short blast of warm air. And the main door clicks shut behind me. I haven't got my key.

LOMEIER: I'm going to go up now.

FATIMA: The door's locked.

KARPATI: What am I doing here? I'm standing in a strange flat beside a sleeping woman who's got practically no clothes on.

FATIMA: No point in ringing Franziska's bell – she's not going to wake up anyway.

KALIL: It's so hot in here.

FATIMA: Nobody's going in or out.

LOMEIER: She's had enough time to get dressed by now. I walk along the corridor in the basement.

KARPATI: I kneel beside her sleeping body. Next to those glowing shoulders. There's a bottle of brandy on the little table by the sofa – it's almost empty.

LOMEIER: The light goes out.

FATIMA: The light goes out in the entrance hall. Nobody's coming with a key. Above me balconies for ten floors and the cloudless night sky.

KALIL: I've got to get out of here.

KARPATI: I take a sip.

LOMEIER: I walk on in the dark towards the stairs.

FATIMA: I'm confronted by a whole panel of bells. Vertical rows of names. Ritzkowsky, Ansorg, Richter, Sadic, Tompson, Körte, Baethge, Behrends, Schlösser, Rieling, Dacanalis –

KARPATI: I touch her short blonde hair. Sorry, I –

FATIMA: Hinrichs, Bartels, Duwel, Sander, Awram, Fischer, Eckstein, Viani duhduh duhduh duhduh. Where do I start? The light in the entrance hall comes back on. Someone might be coming.

LOMEIER: The water goes missing on the seventh floor – and since the sun went down it's roaring through the walls louder than ever.

KARPATI: Before, when you went into the bathroom for a shower, I was standing by the window over there, I saw you.

LOMEIER: Ground floor.

KARPATI: You see – I live in the building opposite and I saw you when you came into the bathroom. The window was open. The sun was being reflected in the little cupboard over the sink with the toothbrushes.

LOMEIER: I put a sign up on the lift door: OUT OF ORDER.

KALIL: I sit on the floor of the lift and stare at the locked inner door.

FATIMA: It's Lomeier – hey!

KARPATI: I could see you – you were turning the taps on. And you, you were so –

FATIMA: Hey!

KARPATI: You were so – how can I describe it –

LOMEIER: Seven flights of stairs.

KALIL: Maybe if I can get the inner door open, something'll happen.

FATIMA: He can't see me!

KARPATI: The window was open and the sun was being reflected in the mirror –

FATIMA: He disappears up the stairs – and he's gone.

KALIL: Maybe then someone might be able to hear me –

KARPATI: And I wanted to kiss you – though I didn't know that yet, not at that point.

FATIMA: She's not going to hear it, but I try anyway: I press our own bell: Dehke/Mansur.

A bell rings.

KARPATI: There's a ring at the bell.

LOMEIER: First floor.

KARPATI: The bell rang but she didn't wake up.

FATIMA: She just goes on sleeping.

KARPATI: She just goes on sleeping.

A long ring at the bell.

FATIMA: Course –

KARPATI: Must be someone downstairs at the main door because the door up here's still open –

LOMEIER: Second floor.

KALIL: I try pushing my fingers through the narrow gap in the inner door.

FATIMA: I look at the whole row from top to bottom. Underneath us, on the sixth floor lives Katja Hartinger, who does her washing in the basement every Friday night. That's how I know her. She's always down in the basement this time on a Friday night. And today's Friday.

KALIL: But the door won't budge. Not even a centimetre.

LOMEIER: You haven't understood anything, have you, anything at all – why am I thinking about this now?

KARPATI: The woman sleeping on the sofa looks uncomplicated, optimistic, curious –

FATIMA: Katja won't open the door. I'll try the Hinrichs next on five. But the husband works nights and she won't open the door if he's not there.

KALIL: I jam my back against the side wall next to all the buttons and try to lever the inner door open with my feet.

LOMEIER: Third floor.

KALIL: Slipped –

KARPATI: As if it might be nice to start off by spending Sunday mornings together, trying out new cafes in town –

KALIL: Try again –

FATIMA: Marion Richter on four usually spends Friday nights in watching TV with her boyfriend Andi. She's bound to be in.

KARPATI: Drinking cafe latte, or latte macchiato.

KALIL: The door's giving.

FATIMA: Or they cook and then have a bath together.

KALIL: But not much.

FATIMA: Come on – I start talking to the intercom, although no-one at all answers. Hello? Hello?

KALIL: Again.

FATIMA: Ring again – Open up.

KALIL: One more go – Get open.

LOMEIER: Fourth floor.

FRANZISKA: My mother's in the kitchen. The lights are on. Late autumn. The painted walls of the stairs outside. My parents' flat when I was little. Everything's special.

KALIL: I kick it as hard as I can. Something breaks. Whatever. The inner door gives way.

FATIMA: Marion's not opening. She's not in and neither's her boyfriend. Or else they really are in the bath together.

KARPATI: Later in the morning we'll wander through the streets. We'll pause in the middle of a little bridge and both look down into the river. What a summer –

KALIL: The inner door's open. To my surprise however I'm not confronted by the bare wall of the lift shaft. I'm standing in front of the metal door on the fifth floor. I can see through its little window into the hallway. But the door won't open. There's a catch of some kind keeping it shut.

FRANZISKA: The children's room is to my left, kitchen and bathroom are on the right, the living room is straight ahead and beyond that is my parents' bedroom. I'm four or five.

LOMEIER: Anything at all – the way she said that.

FATIMA: There's no name by the bell for the third floor, though I'm sure there's someone living there.

KALIL: I can't see the stairs through the window but it sounds like someone's coming up.

LOMEIER: Fifth floor.

FATIMA: I can hear the bell ring on the third floor from down here. They must have the balcony door open. Yes? says a voice on the intercom, a woman. There are voices in the background, music, a party maybe. Hello, look I'm sorry to bother you, I've locked myself out and –

KALIL: Hel-lo?

LOMEIER: Look: you didn't really believe that did you?

FRANZISKA: If I stand on my tiptoes I can just see over the edge of the balcony. There are cars driving past, people walking between buildings.

KALIL: Nobody can hear me.

FATIMA: The woman's talking to me in a foreign language. Hello? I – A crackle. She's hung up. I ring again.

A bell rings.

Wait.

KARPATI: Everything'll be new and different. Special.

FATIMA: Hello? a man asks through the loudspeaker.

KALIL: Hello?

FATIMA: Hello? I've locked myself out and now I'd like to – more voices, music, then nothing.

LOMEIER: Sixth floor. I can't go any further.

KALIL: Nothing.

KARPATI: Her eyes are moving backwards and forwards under her eyelids. She's dreaming.

FRANZISKA: I'm six years old. My parents work for an insurance company. I'm a happy child. I'm going to start school in the Autumn and everything smells of grass. That summer we go on holiday. We're in Turkey. On the beach. Mother rubs cream on my back. The sand is so hot it burns your feet. I've never experienced anything like it.

KARPATI: I watch the vertical stripes of her lips.

FATIMA: The man on the second floor doesn't live there any more, although his name is still on the bell.

Apparently he died there and his daughter found the body. I don't know –

KALIL: If I had a screwdriver I might be able to release the catch – or a pen. I've got a pen in my pocket.

FRANZISKA: On the way home we're in Istanbul, we go in mosques which from a distance look like giant tortoises, we visit the bazaar. The covered bazaar, my father tells me, contains everything you can wish for. My mother tells me to hold her hand, but I run on ahead, a long way ahead, down forked passageways, looking up at the domed ceiling or down at my shoes.

KARPATI: I want to kiss her –

FRANZISKA: Men sit outside the shops drinking tea out of little glasses. My parents aren't behind me any more, I don't know where they are, I've lost them. In front of me, in the middle of the bazaar, outside a cafe of some kind, there's an enormous camel.

LOMEIER: I've made it, seventh floor. That roaring.

KARPATI: I kiss her.

FRANZISKA: Someone puts their hand over my mouth. I can hardly breathe.

KARPATI: My lips on hers, my hand for a moment in her hair.

KALIL: The catch gives way, but it won't open.

LOMEIER: I walk along the corridor towards 7–32. Fatima said I could come back.

FRANZISKA: And someone carries me off. I can see the domed ceiling again. But not my shoes.

KARPATI: But why don't you wake up when I kiss you.

LOMEIER: The corridor sounds like a stream.

FATIMA: The first floor's all dark, I can tell that from here.

A bell rings.

Bremer is the name on the bell, but the Bremers are out. At the cinema maybe. Or wherever – there's not that much choice.

KARPATI: Kiss me.

LOMEIER: The whole corridor sounds like a giant river.

FRANZISKA: The sound of a spring. Water. Almost sounds like birds singing. Distant laughter. It's still early in the morning. My servant Fatima puts a tray down by my bed with tea and ayran. And sesame rings. I'm not six any more. I'm twelve.

KARPATI: Something's pulling at me, dragging me away – tearing at me with all its might – what's happening?

LOMEIER: 7–32. I'm there. Strange – The door's open.

KARPATI: I can't stop it –

FATIMA: The people on the ground floor are called Linhard. Haven't a clue who they are.

LOMEIER: Hello? Is anybody there? Ms Dehke?

FATIMA: The intercom makes a noise. Yes? a woman asks.

LOMEIER: No answer.

KALIL: Finally the catch gives in and the door springs open.

FATIMA: It's me, Fatima Mansur from the seventh floor, I'm really sorry to bother you, I've accidentally locked myself out, would you be willing to open the door for me?

KALIL: I'm out.

LOMEIER: I step inside the flat. Hello?

FATIMA: The door buzzes open. I'm back in the building.

KALIL: Thank you God.

LOMEIER: She's lying there on the sofa. Got almost nothing on, just a towel round her – she's asleep, and no-one else is here. Ms Dehke? There's a bottle of brandy on the little table by the sofa, it's almost empty. The way she's lying there – a film of moisture on her skin. Her short blond hair all sweaty, she's breathing fast, maybe she's dreaming.

KALIL: I run upstairs to Fatima's flat – she's bound to be looking for me.

LOMEIER: I stand beside her, watching her. She's sleeping.

FATIMA: I run back up the stairs to our flat.

LOMEIER: Ms Dehke? She doesn't wake up.

FRANZISKA: I am the lover of Sheikh Al Harad Barhadba, but the Sheikh loves me kindly, like a daughter, I am a virgin. I have been living in the harem inside his palace in the desert city of Kinsh el Sar ever since I was kidnapped in Istanbul. I gaze out of the window with its Moorish screen at the oranges blossoming in the courtyard, the water sprinkler is on. The moisture evaporating into the blue sky. It's beautiful. It's gorgeous.

KALIL: Sixth floor.

LOMEIER: I don't know why, but I suddenly kneel down beside her, touch her bare shoulders –

FRANZISKA: Today is a special day. Today I will turn twenty and later the Sheikh, who I could practically call my father, is going to deflower me. I never think about my old home, my parents, never.

KARPATI: The smell of alcohol fills my head.

LOMEIER: And I kiss her. How long is it since I touched a woman, caressed – I kiss her.

FRANZISKA: But Kafra, the Sheikh's first wife, is so jealous of me, the blonde child, last night she cursed me in front of the whole harem.

FATIMA: First floor.

FRANZISKA: For this the Sheikh has had her beheaded.

LOMEIER: And she carries on sleeping. Nothing happens. I stand up, I can still feel her lips on mine. What's happening, I want to scream at her, what are you doing to me –

KALIL: Seventh floor. I go down the corridor to Fatima's flat. Number 7–32.

LOMEIER: The roaring's so loud. Why don't you wake up? Go on then, sleep, stay asleep on your sofa in your two bedroom flat on the seventh floor, I didn't want to kiss you, it just happened, I want to get out of here, out of flat 7–32, I stagger towards the front door, it's still open –

KALIL: The door's open, that's odd –

LOMEIER: I step over the threshold and am surrounded by glistening light. A hot wind envelops me and sand burns in my eyes.

KARPATI: Someone shouts. Where am I?

FATIMA: Second floor.

KALIL: I go into the flat. Fatima? No-one answers. Hello? I close the door behind me. Fatima?

FRANZISKA: But even disembodied, lying in the dust, her sinister skull still shouts after me one last time: This is your curse. You shall be destroyed. You shall be one of the lost. You shall remember nothing of what you once were. Misfortune is what you shall bring to anyone who kisses your lips, and you shall never see the moon again until one night you become what you truly are.

KARPATI: There's glass all around me. I'm standing in a liquid of some kind. It smells alcoholic. I'm standing in brandy.

KALIL: I walk through the hallway. Lying on the floor are Fatima's keys, with the camel.

LOMEIER: There's sand all around me as far as the horizon.

FRANZISKA: Do something, screams the Sheikh, do something, scream the women.

KARPATI: I'm in a bottle. I'm in the brandy bottle on the little table by the sofa that I just drank out of.

LOMEIER: The sun is high above me.

KARPATI: Through the glass, distorted, enlarged, I can see the woman I just kissed sleeping on the sofa. She's still dreaming. Her eyes are still moving backwards and forwards under her eyelids.

FRANZISKA: Now at long last the executioner's axe halves the severed head vertically right down the middle. Silence.

KALIL: Hello? Is anybody there?

FATIMA: Third floor.

KALIL: On the living room sofa – like she always is when I come – Franziska, Fatima's flatmate, is sleeping.

KARPATI: I'm tiny. My centimetre long shoes are soaked in brandy. Above me the neck of the bottle, which I forgot to record, too high to reach. A breath of air catches in the bottle opening, making a deep note. Hello?

LOMEIER: I'm in a desert. It's so bright, I can hardly open my eyes. I look down at myself – nothing else about me seems to have changed – sandals, grey overall, same as usual. The heat's so dry there isn't a single bead of sweat on my forehead.

KALIL: She's got practically nothing on.

FRANZISKA: What a nightmare.

KALIL: She looks beautiful.

KARPATI: A man has come into the room. He's standing by the sofa.

FRANZISKA: Where am I?

KALIL: She's waking up – hello.

FATIMA: Fourth floor.

FRANZISKA: I'm lying on a sofa in a room. There's a little table beside me. On it there's a bottle of brandy, it's almost empty. I've got practically nothing on, I'm just wrapped in a towel. Where am I? A strange man stands next to me, looking at me. How did I get here?

KALIL: Hello – she seems confused. Maybe she's been dreaming.

KARPATI: How did I get in this bottle –

FRANZISKA: Quickly I look round the room – instead of the Moorish screens there's a big picture window with radiators and blinds. It's night outside. In front of it there's a television standing on a sandy-coloured carpet on the floor. Prints and posters on the walls, next to cheap shelving and photos of people I've never seen before in my life –

KALIL: Is everything alright?

KARPATI: And how am I ever going to get out of here? Help!

LOMEIER: You're not seriously going to go round in that overall all day long, are you?

KARPATI: The woman's woken up, but she can't hear me. The man is next to her, he's enormous. Hello? Can't you see me? I'm in here.

FATIMA: Fifth floor.

LOMEIER: Why not?

FRANZISKA: I can't say a word.

LOMEIER: The thing looks ridiculous. You're ridiculous.

KALIL: She doesn't say anything. I'm Kalil – Fatima's boyfriend. The front door was open. You don't by any chance know where Fatima's gone do you? I got stuck in the lift – on the fifth floor – but I got out. You better not use it in future.

FRANZISKA: He smiles. And talks about a lift.

KARPATI: She stands up, makes sure the towel is covering her and walks to the window. Hello? Can't you hear me?

KALIL: She stands up and walks to the window.

FRANZISKA: I'm standing by the window of a tall building, on the seventh or eighth floor maybe.

KARPATI: She looks out.

FRANZISKA: I grew up in a building like this. A building

like this one was where I spent the first years of my life. Oh God. The moon's shining over the next block, and it feels like years since I've seen it.

KALIL: She's weird.

FATIMA: Sixth floor.

KARPATI: A hollow note in the neck of the bottle –

FRANZISKA: It's like I'm coming apart.

LOMEIER: The wind wails as it scrapes along the jagged ridge of the dunes.

FRANZISKA: I need help.

LOMEIER: You're ridiculous. And you make me ridiculous.

KALIL: Suddenly she throws herself into my arms.

KARPATI: She rushes towards him.

FRANZISKA: Please – save me. I'm about to be destroyed. It's the curse the Sheikh's wife put on me – get me out of here.

LOMEIER: Memories like that set your teeth on edge.

KALIL: What?

FRANZISKA: I don't know you, but don't run away from me. Help me, take me back to the desert city of Kinsh el Sar. Sheikh Al Harad Barhadba will reward you handsomely, just don't leave me alone in this nightmare.

LOMEIER: And I was so proud of showing her everything: the heating, the air conditioning, the incinerator and the lift motors.

KARPATI: She clings on to him –

KALIL: Stop it!

KARPATI: And won't let go.

FRANZISKA: No, please –

KARPATI: The towel slips from her shoulders.

KALIL: Get off –

KARPATI: She's naked.

FATIMA: Seventh floor. I've made it.

FRANZISKA: Stay –

KALIL: What's the matter with you? She's naked and she's clinging to me.

FATIMA: I go down the corridor towards our flat.

KALIL: I try to free myself.

KARPATI: He tries to free himself.

FRANZISKA: Don't go away.

KALIL: Stop it –

FRANZISKA: Please –

LOMEIER: Or were you planning to spend your whole life like this? 'Cos I'm not –

FATIMA: The door's shut. But I left it open.

KARPATI: For a split second she presses her lips to his.

KALIL: She kissed me – I don't know how that could have happened.

FATIMA: Why is the door shut now? I press the bell.

A bell rings.

KARPATI: There's a ring at the bell.

KALIL: There's a ring at the bell.

FRANZISKA: Something's ringing.

KALIL: I try to get to the door.

FRANZISKA: Don't go.

FATIMA: Nothing happens. But I can hear voices in the flat.

KALIL: Let go!

FRANZISKA: Don't!

KARPATI: He frees himself. He runs to the door, she's after him – I can't see them any more.

FATIMA: The door opens.

KALIL: Fatima stands in front of me. Franziska stands behind me, clinging onto me again, naked –

LOMEIER: On the brow of one of the dunes ahead of me, flickering in the heat, the silhouette appears of a Bedouin tent. I head towards it. Because you do everything wrong, she said.

FATIMA: Franziska –

FRANZISKA: There's a woman at the door –

FATIMA: Kalil stands before me – with Franziska behind him, she's naked –

KALIL: There's nothing I can say –

FATIMA: You bastard –

KALIL: No, no –

FRANZISKA: This woman seems familiar –

FATIMA: You little bastard.

KALIL: Don't –

FRANZISKA: Stay with me, please –

FATIMA: He stares at me with great big eyes. I'm going to kill you –

KALIL: Fatima –

LOMEIER: Because you always do everything wrong. My feet are sinking in the sand, I fall over, pick myself back up and keep on going in the direction of the tent.

FATIMA: A knife – I'm going to stab him. I need a knife.

KALIL: She barges past me.

FRANZISKA: The woman barges past us.

KARPATI: A woman comes barging in then disappears into the kitchen.

LOMEIER: The dune's so steep I can hardly move forward.

KARPATI: The woman comes back again.

KALIL: She comes back. She's got a knife in her hand.

FATIMA: He runs away.

KALIL: She's going to kill me.

FRANZISKA: He runs away.

KALIL: She runs after me.

FATIMA: Franziska follows me – naked.

KALIL: I take advantage of my lead and run down the corridor. Help!

FATIMA: I'm going to kill you, you deliberately tricked me out of the flat so you could fuck my flatmate while she was sleeping!

FRANZISKA: I run after them. The woman is shouting.

FATIMA: He's almost reached the stairs.

LOMEIER: I'm almost at the top. I can see the tent in front of me, about another fifteen metres away.

KALIL: They're following me. I run down the stairs.

FATIMA: Stop –

FRANZISKA: What kind of building am I in here?

KARPATI: Nobody comes any more. The flat's empty. I'm alone.

LOMEIER: Hello? Is there anybody there? The wind whistles. It howls and roars, gets snarled up in the canvas.

KALIL: Sixth floor. They've reached the top of the stairs.

KARPATI: Curved by the glass in front of me, the table top. The sandy-coloured carpet. The television. The radiator. The cheap bookshelves. The sofa. Her towel lying on the floor.

KALIL: Behind me, right at the end of the corridor, a door opens to one of the flats. Come in, I hear a woman say, as if she were standing right next to me.

LOMEIER: A woman pulls the cloth door of the tent to one side and beckons me in.

KALIL: I run down the corridor to the flat. I can't go on.

FRANZISKA: Not so fast.

KALIL: Number 6–32. By the bell next to the door it says Hartinger. The door's open.

FATIMA: Sixth floor. He's disappeared. Where's he gone – the bastard must be hiding somewhere.

LOMEIER: I step inside the Bedouin tent. My eyes need time to adjust to the sudden darkness. The woman's standing in the middle of the tent. She's alone.

KARPATI: I'm alone in a bottle in a flat that looks like a thousand other flats.

FRANZISKA: He's gone.

KALIL: I shut the door behind me and take a deep breath. A young woman stands in front of me. I was just going to hang my washing out, she says. And she starts undoing her blouse. Then she turns round and bends down, holding onto the clothes horse. Come.

LOMEIER: The woman looks dreadful. A broad purple scar runs diagonally right across her neck and a second scar bisects her face vertically from the scalp down her nose to her chin.

KARPATI: I know it all: the room, the furniture. I've lived like this myself. Alone. And in a couple.

KALIL: Come on, she says.

FATIMA: Kalil's nowhere to be found. I turn back. It's over.

FRANZISKA: The man's gone. I'm getting cold. The other woman turns round, not saying anything. I follow her. What else can I do –

FATIMA: That's it, it's over.

KALIL: Come here –

KARPATI: The faces drift by on the other side of the glass of the women I was once close to amid furniture like this. Only they've changed so much. They're so old. Now they look like their mothers.

FRANZISKA: Wait –

FATIMA: Forget it.

FRANZISKA: But –

FATIMA: Shut up.

KARPATI: I bang on the glass with my fist. Nothing happens, nothing changes. I remember all the hopes, the new beginnings, the togetherness that was once in those faces, the first kisses, the summer nights together in parks, on terraces and balconies, the generosity, the understanding, that one day vanishes, it's gone, even though you were really counting on each other – in flats like this one, or mine, or like the one I used to have with the walk-in cupboard perhaps, or the one with the weird bathroom we used to laugh about so much.

FATIMA: Seventh floor.

KALIL: I don't want to –

KARPATI: That's horrible: thinking everything's going to be alright, at least this time, and then it's not to be, maybe even turns out worse than it ever was before.

FATIMA: I go down the corridor to our flat.

KARPATI: We simply can't stop revealing our true natures – Everything goes dark.

LOMEIER: It's nice of you to come, says the woman with the scars.

KALIL: But I can't help it –

LOMEIER: What's that roaring noise? Is it the wind? No, she says, you know what it is, it's the water. The water? Yes – What water? The water you've been looking for all day – which is why you're here. The water that's gone missing on the seventh floor? That's right, she says, pursing her doubled lips in mockery. Behind me past the tent's open door a jet of water bursts out of the sand and shoots twenty metres up in the air. The water!

KALIL: She moans so loud she's almost screaming –

LOMEIER: I hear the woman with the scars shout: The water brought you here and now it will carry you to your bride, farewell!

KALIL: She's screaming, she's going to pull the clothes horse over.

LOMEIER: The tent and the woman with it dissolve into thin air right in front of my eyes – what did she mean by that? What bride – no answer.

FATIMA: I'm back in the flat, go to my room, get my bags out and start packing.

FRANZISKA: Where are you going?

FATIMA: Where am I going? Franziska's naked in the doorway of my room. What's that got to do with you? Put some clothes on.

FRANZISKA: I was just asking – perhaps I could come too –

FATIMA: No way. Get out of here. Get dressed. In case you've forgotten: your clothes are in the wardrobe next door.

LOMEIER: The desert is filling with water.

FATIMA: She goes. I pack my things. The same things I must once have stood here unpacking, putting into the cupboard. Just like everyone does with their things and their cupboards. Only I've no idea how I ever got to be here, I can't remember.

LOMEIER: The desert is turning into a river.

FATIMA: One day I stood outside the door downstairs with a key in my hand and knew: I live here now. Here's the letter box, that's the lift, this is how you get to the seventh floor, and here's the sandy-coloured carpet on the floor and the television and the cheap bookshelves, and this is your flatmate Franziska, who always falls asleep and never knows in the evening what happened that morning.

LOMEIER: The desert is turning into a channel, a straits. I'm holding the railing of a ferry across the Bosphorus. Ahead of me lie the minarets of Istanbul. I've been here before. On our honeymoon. Twenty-four years ago. D'you remember? a woman's voice asks me. Standing on my right there's a woman who looks like Helga, my first wife, she's wearing the same clothes she had on then, she looks absolutely unchanged, except on her face there's a broad vertical scar from her scalp down her nose to her chin –

FATIMA: I grab the things out of the cupboard, dresses, trousers, sweaters, T-shirts and so on, the lot.

KALIL: She rolls over on her back and I'm on top.

FATIMA: While I'm doing it I think about Kalil. I think about him cheating on me with my flatmate.

FRANZISKA: Who can that man have been who was here earlier?

KALIL: This has got to stop –

FRANZISKA: In the room the woman sent me into, there's a wardrobe.

LOMEIER: Do you still remember how you came to see me – because of a flood in my flat on the seventh floor. It was the middle of the night in summer and a full moon shone brightly over the roofs of the tower blocks, which were brand new. You hadn't expected anyone to call you at that time. Eventually you got the situation under control, the whole flat had been drenched in water coming down from upstairs and you stood there on the balcony with your sleeves rolled up – it was before you got the overall. Maybe you'd had quite different plans for that evening, just never admitted it when we talked about how we'd met. That's nice. Remembering how you met. Or the first kiss. Remember? You went out on to the balcony for a smoke, and suddenly I thought you were so beautiful – so strong and at the same time so forlorn, I thought: he's the one, the one I want to spend the rest of my life with, him, and no-one else. That was the first time I kissed you – beneath a full moon on the balcony on the seventh floor.

FRANZISKA: I open the wardrobe.

LOMEIER: You're not here, I shout, you can't be, why are you persecuting me – leave me alone!

KALIL: I tear myself away from her.

FATIMA: It's stuffy. I go over to the window.

FRANZISKA: The clothes in the wardrobe seem familiar –

KALIL: Don't stop, she yells, I stagger to the door, come back, she yells –

LOMEIER: I didn't do anything, she says – all I want is for you not to be unfaithful to me – leave me alone, I go berserk, I take the electric screwdriver I always carry in the breast pocket of my overall and jab it deep into her eyes, both of them, I keep on stabbing again and again. But all she says is a gentle oh, and then she laughs – and then she vanishes – exactly like –

KALIL: Don't stop, she cries – then when I open the front door she begins howling like a wolf.

FRANZISKA: A blouse, a skirt, narrow yet comfortable shoes – everything seems to fit –

FATIMA: A howl drifts through the flats at night. A cry like the cry of a wolf or a she-wolf.

KALIL: I escape along the corridor and more or less dive down the stairs. The howling can be heard on every floor.

FRANZISKA: These clothes belong to a lab technician, a hospital laboratory assistant.

FATIMA: That's a woman screaming.

LOMEIER: You ought to know, says a woman on my left, we've been here before, twenty-four years ago, and the man with her nods. With our daughter, who we lost then –

FATIMA: I'm packed.

KALIL: Fifth floor. Behind me, right at the end of the corridor, the door to one of the flats opens.

FRANZISKA: With every piece of clothing I put on, my memory becomes clearer: I work as a lab technician. I work in a hospital, every day from nine to five.

KALIL: Come in, I've been waiting for you, I hear a woman say, as if she were standing right next to me. I don't want to, but I run down the corridor to her flat anyway.

LOMEIER: We lost her, the woman says, here in Istanbul, in the bazaar, twenty-four years ago – a blonde child, we've neither seen nor heard from her since, it's like she never existed. And she shakes her head.

FATIMA: That's the lot.

KALIL: Hinrichs is written by the bell. The door's open. She's standing there.

FATIMA: I'm not taking anything else.

KALIL: Hello, she says – Ms Hinrichs. She must be in her late thirties.

FRANZISKA: My job is mainly analysing blood samples. Most of the work's done by machines.

KALIL: And as she does so she loosens the belt round her dressing gown –

FATIMA: I'm off. But I'm going to take the knife with me, just in case I bump into that bastard Kalil on the stairs.

FRANZISKA: And that woman just now was Fatima, who I've been sharing this flat with for years, I'm not sure exactly how long, where is she? Why am I standing here half-dressed in front of the wardrobe? Fatima?

KALIL: She's got nothing on underneath.

LOMEIER: The man with the woman at the railing says: though perhaps it was for the best. Think how much money that child would have cost over the years, her education alone, all the things we couldn't have afforded. The travelling – And then he gives me his card: Helmut Dehke, insurance salesman.

FATIMA: My keys with the camel on are still lying on the floor near the door where I dropped them when I came in with the shopping. No idea why I've got so many keys – seem to be enough for a whole palace.

KALIL: She moans really loud –

FATIMA: Am I going to say goodbye to Franziska?

LOMEIER: The sun dips down behind the Golden Horn and the Süleymanie, it's dark.

FATIMA: What's the point? I close the door to the flat behind me and walk down the corridor. That howling noise is still wafting through the building.

LOMEIER: The ferry railing is on top of a block of flats. I'm standing by the window in a building like mine. I've been here before, I know I have, it's so stuffy here, there's no-one on the sofa, but there on the little table is the bottle of brandy, it's almost empty. I pick it up, I need some fresh air, fresh air, a drink and a cigarette.

KARPATI: I come to. Something's swinging me backwards and forwards. I'm soaked in brandy, I bang my head on the glass, I can hardly breathe – someone's carrying the bottle.

FATIMA: No idea where I'm going to go.

LOMEIER: I head for the balcony.

KARPATI: The floor whizzes past underneath me – the sandy coloured carpet, the hallway, the lino in the kitchen…

LOMEIER: The shopping bags are still there from before –

KARPATI: …the doorframe for the balcony, concrete.

LOMEIER: Beneath me lie the flats. I'm standing by the rail on the balcony. Cigarette. A peculiar howling echoes through the building – what can that be? And where have I just been? Only now do I notice that I'm still holding the card the man on the ferry gave me: Helmut Dehke, insurance salesman.

FRANZISKA: Where's Fatima?

KALIL: No.

LOMEIER: I could do with a drink –

KARPATI: Oh my God.

KALIL: Maybe –

LOMEIER: – maybe not. Someone's coming.

KARPATI: Someone is holding me and the bottle over the edge of the balcony.

FATIMA: When I reach the stairs I look back down the corridor: the pipes in the walls are working – maybe the eighth, ninth and tenth floors have got their water back again.

FRANZISKA: There's someone on the balcony.

LOMEIER: It's Franziska Dehke.

FRANZISKA: Oh, it's Lomeier, the caretaker, he must still be here because of the water pressure. He's smoking.

KARPATI: It's a seven floor drop down there and the only thing between me and it is the glass at the bottom of the bottle.

KALIL: This is not what I want.

LOMEIER: She comes over and stands next to me.

FATIMA: I go down the stairs. The howling gets louder with every step.

KALIL: Out of here. She tries desperately to hold onto me, but I push her away. Down on her knees, she shouts: what are you doing to me?

KARPATI: Beneath me, the streetlamps, the courtyard in front of the building, parked cars, the bus stop.

FRANZISKA: Beautiful evening, isn't it? The moon's so bright.

KARPATI: Listen!

LOMEIER: You've woken up.

FRANZISKA: I – did I – I don't know – how long have you been here?

LOMEIER: A few minutes maybe.

FRANZISKA: Well?

KALIL: I get to the front door. She stays where she is and begins to howl like a wolf.

KARPATI: In the pool of light from one of the streetlamps there's a group of kids smoking. I can hear them laughing.

LOMEIER: Well what?

FRANZISKA: Have you found out anything?

LOMEIER: Like what?

KALIL: The corridor back to the stairs –

FRANZISKA: I mean have you found out yet where the missing water's been going on the seventh floor –

LOMEIER: Oh – yeah.

FRANZISKA: Yeah?

LOMEIER: Yeah.

FATIMA: Sixth floor. Howling's getting louder all the time. It's everywhere now. What was that? I stop.

KALIL: I go down the stairs.

LOMEIER: She looks so new.

FRANZISKA: He leans on the balcony rail and looks at the flats in the night. In his hand he's holding the brandy bottle out of the living room, it's almost empty.

LOMEIER: You were really fast asleep –

FRANZISKA: Aha –

LOMEIER: She leans on the balcony rail next to me and looks at the flats in the moonlight. More homes than you can count, with lights on behind the curtains. She doesn't seem to be aware of the fact that I kissed her.

FRANZISKA: I had a weird dream.

KALIL: Fourth floor. Behind me, right at the end of the corridor, the door to one of the flats opens.

LOMEIER: Did you? The night's warm. No more roaring noise. Just howling. Sounds like a desert wind.

KARPATI: A howl drifts through the night, almost as if a wind is catching in the neck of the bottle, but it's not that –

KALIL: Come to me, a woman says in my ear, as if she were standing right next to me.

FRANZISKA: Yeah. I dreamt that a man kissed me in my sleep and then vanished – I don't know where to – a Bedouin tent, the inside of a bottle like that one, I can't remember any more.

KALIL: I don't want to, but I walk down the corridor to the flat with the open door anyway.

FATIMA: Fifth floor.

KALIL: Marion Richter's what it says by the bell.

KARPATI: He plays nervously with the bottle in his hand. If he lets go of me now, if the bottle were to slip out of his fingers, I'd drop down seven floors to my death.

KALIL: I can't help it – I go inside.

LOMEIER: I'd forgotten all about the brandy bottle in my hand. Look, I'm sorry for just helping myself, but –

FRANZISKA: Please, you're welcome, if you've still got to work at this time, then the least you can do –

LOMEIER: I didn't actually want any –

KALIL: Hello, says the woman standing before me in the hallway. I'm Marion. I was just going to have a bath. Or would you rather watch TV? My boyfriend Andi's not here tonight. Or do fancy a meal first?

FRANZISKA: And then everything filled up with water, and there was a man near me in the living room, whose lips I accidentally touched, but he ran away. Why am I telling him this?

KALIL: Come on, let's go into the kitchen.

LOMEIER: She stands beside me, glancing at me from time to time, unsure of herself. She's pretty.

KARPATI: I don't want to die –

FRANZISKA: He's good-looking. Why didn't I ever notice that before. It's just the overall looks a bit naff.

KALIL: The woman starts taking her clothes off in front of the fridge.

FATIMA: Fourth floor.

FRANZISKA: Would you mind taking your overall off?

LOMEIER: Er – no, of course not, why, is it bothering you?

FRANZISKA: I just wanted to –

LOMEIER: It's fine – I take off my overall, tucking the card out of sight into a pocket. How can I explain that to her –

KARPATI: Please –

FATIMA: I carry on further down the stairs.

KARPATI: Oi!

FRANZISKA: Wait, let me help you, I'll hold the bottle.

LOMEIER: No, it's alright.

KARPATI: He puts the bottle down on the narrow balcony rail and takes off his overall. If either of them knocks the bottle now, I'm dead.

LOMEIER: There.

FRANZISKA: I just wanted to see what you look like without your overall on.

FATIMA: Something's not right. I turn round and go back up the stairs.

LOMEIER: She's smiling.

FRANZISKA: You probably had very different plans for tonight, rather than looking for a leak in the water pipes.

KALIL: She moans.

LOMEIER: You mean I'd have gone out tonight – no, definitely not.

FRANZISKA: You can admit it…I won't ask who with. He laughs. He's strong and so –

KARPATI: I press my face against the glass. Why can't you see me?

FATIMA: Fourth floor. What's that? I go along the corridor.

LOMEIER: I like her.

FRANZISKA: So forlorn. I want to kiss him.

LOMEIER: If she'd kiss me now –

FATIMA: Marion Richter in 4–32's door's not shut properly. Why?

FRANZISKA: He turns towards me.

LOMEIER: She makes a move towards me.

FATIMA: I step inside.

KARPATI: He turns to face her. At the same time, she moves towards him.

FATIMA: I'm standing in the hallway of someone else's flat. There are noises coming from the kitchen.

FRANZISKA: My elbow accidentally brushes against the brandy bottle that's still standing on the balcony rail.

KARPATI: She brushes the bottle with her elbow. The bottle tips.

KALIL: She's moaning really loud.

KARPATI: The bottle tips over the edge of the railing into the air. I'm falling. The bottle plummets seven floors. I'm hurtling down seven floors.

FATIMA: I'm standing in the kitchen of someone else's flat. The layout is the same as Franziska's kitchen. Kalil and Marion Richter are by the fridge in front of me. She's naked. And he – they don't notice me. She's moaning.

KARPATI: Sixth floor. There's a woman on the balcony howling at the moon. The pavement hurtles towards me. At the same time everything happens very slowly.

LOMEIER: She's standing right in front of me.

FRANZISKA: I'm right up close to him.

FATIMA: I'm standing behind them. They don't see me.

KARPATI: Fifth floor. There's a woman on the balcony howling at the moon. The lights in the windows turn to stripes.

LOMEIER: I hardly dare breathe.

FRANZISKA: I lay my hands carefully on his chest.

KALIL: The kitchen clock's ticking. There are coloured magnets stuck to the door of the fridge.

LOMEIER: She lays her hands carefully on my chest.

FATIMA: I slam the knife into his back.

KALIL: She screams. What's that? Blood in her face.

KARPATI: Fourth floor. A woman is stabbing a man.
There's blood on the window pane.

FATIMA: I am the servant of Sheikh Al Harad Barhadba.
I'm standing in the courtyard of his palace in the desert
city of Kinsh El Sar. It's a clear night. The branches of
the orange trees cast blue shadows. In my hands I hold
a kitchen knife, but where are the keys to the countless
doors of this great house? I always carry them with me –

LOMEIER: She kisses me.

FRANZISKA: He kisses me.

KARPATI: Third floor. A party. Music.

KALIL: What's that?

FRANZISKA: It's my first ever kiss.

KARPATI: Second floor. Darkness.

LOMEIER: We kiss. For the first time. I hold her as tight
as I can.

KARPATI: First floor – I'm dead.

FRANZISKA: We kiss. I close my eyes, and I can still feel
the moonlight.

*KARPATI screams. KALIL screams. A bottle drops from
the flies and smashes on stage.*

The End.